Somewhere Between the Stem & the Fruit

Somewhere Between the Stem & the Fruit

Poems

Gwen Frost

Broadstone

Library of Congress Control Number 2020936781
ISBN 978-1-937968-62-5

Design by Larry W. Moore

Cover artwork by Leah Cromett,
used by permission.
Author photo by Anna Del Savio,
used by permission.

Broadstone Books
An Imprint of
Broadstone Media LLC
418 Ann Street
Frankfort, KY 40601-1929
BroadstoneBooks.com

For David Hillis, who showed me the world of poetry,
and thus saved my life.

You listened
at a crucial time
for me to be heard.

You were the first person to call me a poet.

Thank you for believing in me;
this book happened
because you did.

CONTENTS

PART THREE

PART ONE

THERE ARE MANY WAYS TO TELL THIS STORY

I meet the lip of the ocean:
the untraversable distance
we have placed between us.

A palm shaped leaf pressed to the throat:
the Teeth in the mouth of a sixteen year-old girl,
ripping from their homes forever.

That was your only crime:
Vacancy

A cavity I filled
by raising myself

        again.

CRADLE

I can't see my newborn baby, but she smells like pink and newspaper
like my friend drinking espresso saying she will fall in love tonight
I can't smell my newborn baby
but she looks like roses
like my sister telling me she wishes she could stay
in these moments
longer
she looks like the sky opening and closing
for wings
looks like the breathing seafoam and bone sand
I can't hear my newborn baby
but she sounds like touching your curls
like octopi sucking up color
from boat graves in the bottom of the ceiling
I can't see her yet
but I feel her in morning
in pools of footprints on water and ripples across white walls
I can't hear my newborn baby
but she smells like the sacrificial ashes
from a bonfire puzzle of corsets
    I will burn her a bridge to cross over
I can't see my newborn baby
but when
I do,
she is sniffing across the field for brown mice
birds of prey above, circling skin from bone
corn husks papering their feathers
and for the first time ever
I am not scared
because for the first time ever
the birds are not here
for me.

WILLOW

I'm the Jeffrey Dahmer of paper
making you into objects that fill my room
my lampshade, my teeth, my voice
belong to you
(at times.)
The Creating of you into many little pieces, a dismemberment into small sheets;
I christen this poem Murder.

The skin cells you shed in my sweaters drop like seeds
sprouting a mess of weeds and growths across my bedroom floor.
My paper greenhouse shivers under your windstorm of stray hairs.

I do not wait for you to die
to keep you alive
with altars of objects alienated from your control,
even your scent is not yours,
   it is You.

I do not wait for you to die
to mourn you.

I want to be enough for all the girls I love.
Sandpaper shaving away my breasts, pouring cement into my negative space,
I want to be enough for all the girls I love, but I feel cavernous
like all the scaffolding doesn't sound or surround
something hospitable. They want a kingdom.
(I want to be) all the girls I love.
I want a forest flood, a paper shredder, I want
a body that could make you see my love as real.

I've built you into furniture
but I just can't seem to love you domestically enough.

And, even
    if
        I
       could,

I don't know
if you would *let* me.

Again, with stanzas, I've made you
into so many little pieces,
a dismemberment of you;
I christen this poem Revenge.

12. GOD

    Wanting to feel holy dipping two fingers in a bowl of grey,
wanting to know I did   the right thing
for her. Dragging these ghosts
on my heels I ask:
why can't I lose anything on *purpose* ?
Resentment keeps crawling through my front door
while my lost cat is coughing up blood in some alley.
I need a cat-door too small for ghosts but big enough for a purring skeleton
the too-small-but-big-enough game,
the Fathers singing into their boots "You shouldn't run *from*, only *towards*."
Obviously they have never been fucking scared.
When I'm sitting at the pyre, drinking all the sink water,
I pray, I pray for her domesticated liberty, hoping it is not so grand
as to kill her.
And if it was so grand, I would pray her
the death of freedom, total and true submission,
the admittance of mortality I have so long denied her
with my syringes and creams.
I hope you know I wanted to keep you, safe, did I keep you
safe or enslaved
I want the best for you!
I want to be
what is best for you.
If you didn't want to do something as intimate as die
while in capture, I can't blame you.
God is coincidence, not absurdity.
The intention
behind a straight line, is hidden, the line ends and starts in the same place,
the boots run from, run toward,
I saved her
from the life I didn't think she should have.
She was running neither from nor toward.

She was running.
She was God.

Still is, probably.

TICK

I had a dream about firefly plankton, meadow particulates
braiding through the breath of an afternoon kitchen.

You weren't sick anymore.
You looked like the first day I saw you.
You looked like characters do in movies
before the plot wears them down.
                              tick tick tick tick tick tick tick tick tick tick tick tick
In my dream you were a World, painting
trumpets with words, my ear to your spine
while your heart beat warm blood.
I didn't feel like you were about shatter
the way I feel all the time now.
                              tick tick tick tick tick tick tick tick tick tick tick tick
In my dream, you started singing again.
You had always liked to sing.
a eulogy for your dead selves: "She had always liked to sing."
My sealed heart screaming
     Survive, or Don't.
I'm sick of this unbearable 'almost.'
                              tick tick tick tick tick tick tick tick tick tick tick tick
You, dangling by a thread in front of me,
twisted trapeze performance, your tortuous grace.
I wonder how you got pulled up like that.
I want to accuse you of building yourself
so breakable, of playing the part too well.
tick tick tick tick tick tick   tick tick tick tick tick tick

Waking moments I spend
kissing the bathroom tiles on which you kneel,
plugging holes in your throat with flesh yardsticks and scotch tape.
I taste you kissing your insides back to the ocean,
your garbage-disposal'd dinner fighting to reassemble itself.
I say
     You can only give so much of yourself
yet I wait for you on the bottom of the ocean floor,
eyes bulging and mouth glub glubbing,

wishing I could hear the advice I tell.
tick tick tick tick tick tick tick tick tick tick tick tick

But in my dream, we are laying on the grass and it is Spring.
You're murmuring poems about oranges and Light and brilliance.
Your precious form is radiating, solid. I am braiding our friend's hair,
she is humming. Even the trees have begun to take the sun for granted.
Here, I don't take you for granted. People walk past us and see
cooing mermaids in love, blooming in a sea of Good Health.

My mind's projector sk ips/tick/ c l i c k s /tick/ *whirs* / blacks out

tick   tick   ti

Looking around it is all wrong. You're gone
tick tick tick tick tick tick tick tick tick tick tick tick
it is dark here in my bed.
It is
Beneath   the bottom of the Ocean,
            where all the vomit goes, where a mermaid would never swim to,
                  where friends don't get better, a place the sun can't bear to illuminate.

Rigid teeth and dry lips, the clock tick-ticking in the hallway.
tick metric interruptions of my moments of now *tick tick tick ticktick ticktickick*

                  I can't undo the whisper
                        you've become.

            dream is memory, memory is Eulogy, this dream is Eulogy:
                  You had always liked to sing.
tick tick tick tick tick tick tick tick tick tick tick tick

9

A Temporary Solution to a Permanent Problem

The Interweaving of Two Pantoums

We are the same in this place.
Drowning is falling slowly
"technically, she was falling before her feet left the ledge,"
somewhere between the stem and the fruit, suspended in non-gravity.

     Somewhere between life and death, between green and blue,
     this place of being more alive than we are dead.
     Is it possible to approach this point
     without solid ground to jump from?

Drowning is falling slowly
dragged up down and to both sides
Somewhere between the stem and the fruit, suspended in non-gravity
ripping the floor of outer space.

     This place of being more alive than we are dead,
     of all our prayers answered   too late,
     without solid ground to jump from.
     It is the sound of one hand clapping.

Dragged up, down, and to both sides
handless fingers in my eye sockets, pulling,
ripping the floor of outer space
I am rendered silent by these contradictions,

     of all our prayers answered too late.
     Immobile due to chaos, the body floats,
     it is the sound of one hand   clapping.
     Is it possible to come back from this?

Handless fingers in my eye sockets, pulling.
"Technically, she was falling before her feet left the ledge…"
I am rendered silent by these contradictions:
We are the same in this place.

Immobile due to chaos, the body floats
Is it possible to approach this point,
is it possible to come back from this?
Somewhere between life and death, between green and blue,
        somewhere between the stem and the fruit:

        We are the same in this place.

This is what you ask of me

To lay me down on a field of rose cubes,
ice petals, to harvest the golden wheat
bursting through my scalp.
To swallow you
back into the womb:
  This is what you ask of me.

To cradle you at my breast and part your lips with my nipple,
unbraiding my legs and fingers to shade the skin on your cheeks and chest.
To behave as the weeping widow, who umbrellas her hair over the front lawn,
curtaining you from the weather you can't predict:
  This is what you ask of me.

> The only time I am a God to you is when you fall to your knees,
> praying that I will peel apart my rib cage to offer the beating
>   pomegranate.
> Don't you think I know how your hands shake
> Don't you think I see how truths and teeth sink through your hands
> when the words bleed too heavy?

To draw you
a bath, draw you water, draw you silk.
To put coconut in your hair and lemon behind your ears.
To draw your portrait, you say
        "It must be both beautiful and true."
  This is what you ask
  of me, but it doesn't ever feel like a question.

To fill you in
To give you detail
To scribe story and forgiveness across the calluses of your palms
  and this
  is what is asked
  Of me,
        but don't you think I know
        how empty you become
        when I am not looking at you?

EUTHENASIA

Can you define something strictly by what it is *not* ?
I want to be like this pumpkin
on my kitchen table I want
to be fucking useless
please
carve out my insides gut my seeds
with your fingers get me under your
nails cut a face onto my unembellished
skin light a small white candle and set it gently
in my stomach.
I will lighthouse your domestic gate, glowing from blocks away,
swallowing smoke and sitting sedentary,
a lantern anchor beckoning,
a monster carved into my smile.
    I only scare you   because you made me so.
Maybe I'd rather sit rotting on your steps
than next to a thousand of the Unpicked.
Like the trophy puppy chosen over her brothers,
she is sticking her tongue out at them, the bitch,
no she is panting, she is smiling, no she is baring her
teeth, she wanted to be abducted I mean adopted:
A point of existence,
which was only to be chosen.
A puppy or a pumpkin or a wife
rotting into compost with the other Excess.
Maybe I'd rather die in a field
than in your arms.

WATCH

What makes a good film?
"Torture the women," said Alfred Hitchcock.
A promise to be sensational,
to be obscene,
on time,
like kissing,
and the ripping apart
of teenage girls.
What makes a *good* movie?
It is the overpowering of bodies,
wolves yelling "harder" at textual rape, at sexual evidence.
Cinema-bitten erecting of hair on skin, pulled until
spectacle tears,
then the cum
ripped out of eyes.
It is the fetish, which is only   what is excessive—
to love, to fetishize, to focus, essentialize the sum into a
single object   of affection.
I do not think these victimizations are different, women crying and cumming
and cut-up, the bad-good girl,
she always bleeds the same shit, regardless of virginal status
Torture the women!
It takes torture to become a woman,
as castration suggests. There is no feminine equivalent,
as if you could not rob someone of the female sex,
you could not rob a woman of herself.
Hitchcock, these are not stories.
I fear your emperor fantasy of hereditary domination,
I fear the fiction you wrote that people live every day.
I'd slit your throat for your confidence
in describing the hearts you'd like to break
I'd unmake you
because I'd like to be as you are—
sowing, planting, leaving, always leaving.
But my roots grow from my womb to the soil
and I am so tired of seeing men fly overhead
with their cocky necks and spitting members.

I want to be loving someone back to a line of blue milk
instead of pedalling into an exit or
a line dividing two things into   two.
Entirely human monsters lie not on a side, but on the very line.
I don't know why you chose to kill women and not yourself
but I know there was a line running through your choice.
I know what makes a good movie, but
why do you need a knife when you already have a penis?

Turns out, there are a million different ways to kill a girl.

SKIN OF

Joan of Arc as a wickless candle, wax statue of a dream,
how much detail was necessary to make you real? I worry
that when I split open your fingers, I will find only
poisoned oxygen, or worse: stuffing. I know the Lesson,
that Heroes get remembered and Legends never die
but all I can think of is melting 100 candles to cover
my body in a protective armor of beeswax. What is the
difference between being a Hero and looking like one?
My wax could teach me to sit in the shade, like the
Mothers in Hawaii with their books, their kids furiously
burning their skin and calories, the Mothers in
the shade wearing sun hats (in the name of all that is unnecessary).
Legends never die but Heroes do. You can't even be a Hero if you
don't die, the lesson reads in reverse, but Joan, you are not different
from the Backpacks descending from bridges, nametag tombstones on
the empty Seats in classrooms, (in the name of all that is unnecessary).
In the name of all that is unnecessary,
I wonder what I could have done differently.
I find it hard to believe that my wax armor would not
have saved them all. Joan, they built you a Legend, not a Hero
like the name tags, your stare forever fixed on battle.
I trace your dry gaze eyes cold hands fixed
polished skin bitter strength stiff joints…
immortalized, but not alive.

I'd choose death
over the Forever
you are condemned to.

Leftovers

My sister and I took turns playing
the invisible child my mother gave birth to.
Acting invisible has less to do with matter
and more to do with the way matter *moves*.

See-through teeth smiles
bit by bit we alternated fading away in her eyes
hair bows dropped to the ground
from where heads should have been.

Being invisible means no current
absolute transcending stillness.
The invisible are above the ghostly tasks
of slamming doors and going bump in the night.

The invisible don't even know they are there.

As air crawls up my arms, devouring cell after mole after hair,
abducting blood with wind, our names reduced to whispers,
I lock eyes with my sister.
Or I think I do.

But once you have made yourself Nothing
for someone,
so many times,
the ashes don't unburn as easily.

Your bodies erase from their positions in pictures,
reimagined backgrounds of what could have been if you had   *never.*
And now, scattered as you are,
the air cannot tell herself apart
from your Nothing.

THE BARREL OF THE WOUND'S ORIGIN

I carved my hair down
to the scalp with my best friend's scissors
trying to find the bullseye painted
on the back of my skull.
No evidence of paint, hands or a brush.
I could have sworn
there were people there were beetles
on rooftops in alleys under bridges
shining their red lights on my achilles.

I wake up hungover from the paranoia I imbibed
I wait to feel
human wait for relief from
the eyes bloodying my back wait
to sweat this obsession from my pores.
the Withdrawal whispers that sobriety will mean giving up paranoia
        (how will I know when to run)
the Withdrawal whispers that survival will mean a five-foot arm
        (how will anyone get close to me)
the Withdrawal whispers, but it is lost in the wind
of the Siren song, wailing her parasitic trap.

In my eyelids sailors drown as they claw
at the crests of waves, trying to grasp
the mermaid's matted golden hair, a net to catch meat and men,
her seashell breasts slicing the drapery of her ribs.
But I'm no mermaid I doggy paddle
I am Lillith;
meant to be the wife of Adam
but in my refusal to be subservient,
I am banished to the Red Sea.
the Bible forgets me from the story
like it forgot all the women
who were neither an apple nor a snake.

Unable to flourish into a sea goddess,
I sink

I sink

so I take another drink.

One morning the bullseye was still dripping red.
I ravaged for the wound's barrel, and dug up
a paintbrush from under my bed.
It was made of the stems my head bore, my discarded feminine mane,
still wet from drink—

and completely free of prints.

The Gift

"A strawberry is not a nipple," She hears in her mother's voice.
Something green is not something red, water is not milk,
but her body blossomed produce anyway,
the fatty ducts poisoned by root systems of nectar.

This is The Gift.

Some superpowers develop in puberty, but changing bodies never change
the same. Her bra held an impossible farmers market, kumquats, figs,
blueberries, she rolled over in bed and thoughtlessly made jam.
Her breast plate humbled every peach farmer in the county. Dress after dress bled
through, tie-dyed with pulps and sugar, azure, magenta red red red.
The whole town latched at the teet of her growths,
their urine semen unseasonably sweet, the surrounding fields
rotting with non-magic.
But the wonder and awe only tranced them for so long.

Then, the Fear.

"The world needs a hero," she hears in her mother's voice.
The Gift could have solved world hunger, and it would have, and shouldn't it be so?

"All she needs is three meals a day," her mother's voice tells the footsteps approaching her room. Three meals cost much less than maintaining fields and paying workers, and when something wonderful costs very little, it must be hidden.

The Coats poked and prodded her veins, dissecting her genetic makeup, asking her body how it was built, asking it how to build more of her. She becomes The File, a mutated accident born of some God's cruel fingers. Under the fluorescent lights, the fruit turned bulbous, inedible, rotten. A peach rolled from her bed to the linoleum floor and burst, vomiting ants.

This is The Gift.

While walking to her favorite Cafe on C street, she was trampled by fans and phantoms, grabbing at her flesh breast fruit, consumed, cracking two of her ribs. If enough people love you, you are not Free. She wondered at times if She was being praised or prosecuted.

Both can be dangerous.
Goddess or Mutant.
Both can be dangerous.

To be always creating is exhausting, her lungs crushed more and more beneath the always-coming harvest, her wheezing machinery rusting with sugar and estrogen.

The Gift from no God.

Something green holds shades of red, a nipple is a strawberry, but not the other way around, and *didn't she want to be needed?*

How wretched we build Gods, how lonely the Pedestal.

As She fell asleep in her Garden bed Grave,

She wondered if Aliens were born on Earth.

THE SCAPEGOAT

In a true effort to be unbreakable
I hid my X-rays somewhere they wouldn't exist.
Anything hiding under your bed is imaginary,
my Mother always told me,
so I hid them unreal.
Pretending my bones
never split I became convinced
they never could.
Phantom pains of ghost injuries
gaslighting my nerves (it never happened) it never happened
but the scratches on the backs of
my arms
hissed over my denials.
First, I tried to drown them,
my X-rays,
in the McKenzie River.
I held their lying heads under water
my knuckles turning blue around throats of photos.
the current making herself Held by paper lungs.
A deer across the river raises her head.
She asks me to stop, and then she is gone.
Feet thrashing, undoing the glass of the surface with their idiotic, spastic legs
my hopes levitated at the waning bubbles, the quiet that pooled in my ear cavities.
I was unbreakable.
But the next morning
I found my immortal evidence of weakness
washed up at the foot of my bed, the X-rays, dry as bones.
Wails crawled up the stairs—
I found my Mother, sobbing over wet fur.
She found our two cats
sisters
drowned in the bathtub
wet tails like river snakes.
She said "they must have fallen asleep,"
said that "something so gruesome must have been an accident."
Our dog stood in the doorway
and raised her head.

She couldn't speak, or beg me to confess,
but I knew she would never look at me
the same way again.

PART TWO

WILLOW II

At times,
to mourn you,
I open the window
into a body,
a body that could have kept you
from our premature death,
how our nubile companionship
dropped from a tense string.
I keep misreading bare as brave.
I keep misreading all of it.

                       Losing you
                       took my voice.

But my lampshade,
my teeth,
my little pieces
of paper,
those,
you let me keep.

OCEAN PRAYER

my lungs beat loudly, beach folding-chair outside-in,
rusty Monarch, careful steps...

and I thought, being married is like
tin goblets of bathwater
those slow, blue blinks
and the return of bodily brain
trudging through low blackouts,
both of us held by the State.

Father me back to forgiveness,
blood the oaks into their homes

Survival (of anything)
is strangled by the Forever of When.
The permanence,
only, of When.
Can it be prevented?

Not forever.
Wine swallowed glass, and blood did ice.
We were raised so differently
but found a way   to Love   the same
for a second of 'not forever,'   the same.
Your noble heart a whirlpool of deep sea church bells.
My anxious lungs holding holy tales of Possible.
But it can't be prevented,

the future. Not forever. The glass will melt,
the ice will tapeworm back into the bottoms of feet,
bloody wine and bleeding grapes will run like bathwater.

A monarch with wet wings married to porcelain—
where do I return in moments of immobility?

Unweaving images into thread of skin, I braid my fingers into your
        skullcap clothing.
In this segment, some blind priest possessed no comfort
in the burning of doors that held our mirrors:
        Mirrors can close the Universe if their tongues touch.
        What connects head & brain, blood & glass, eyelid & lung, you & I?

There are places without gravity.

Where will I return in moments of wet wings
if it is not

        downwards?

STRUNG OUT

my mouth carries a cheese grater
stuttering down the sides of my fingers

leaving shredded petals by my toes.
  my front teeth scrape down the nails, wetting the metal with anxiety.

i watch my un-mummified corpses drudging down the flesh on your
chest,
i watch the fingers crawl through time towards my mouth, but i can't keep
      them away,

if only i had another hand.
  Father slaps the fingers to safety, away from

my ravenous beak bearing knives of bone.
  disciplined, i fall

still. hands follow bodie's suit and play
  dead

    i watch from my friends eyes as my fingertips drag along the pavement
      dribbling their brushstrokes over the cleanest pages

  the nibbling of my hands fills the room

Mom says "chew with your mouth closed,"
      Autophagia is impolite

  but i peel the skin from my fingers like string cheese
swallowing saliva and rinds, white pulp of my husks

      when my members erupt polluted tentacles
        and burst iron clouds of embarrassed humanity into my mouth, the
            taste whimpers

                              "you've gone too far again"

i want to forget. if only i had another hand.

   i try to part my thighs with these damaged pliers and my legs look up,
        scowling at me

  their pleas carved in livid blue and violent violet.

my legs and fingers are truly exhausted of loving me.

i hear them whispering at night when they think i am asleep
hear them complaining of how i've betrayed them, over and over

how i am foolish, an abusive lover,

undeserving of being the owner of such functional extremities,

they hiss they   hiss

"selfish cannibalistic bitch"

how i hate them

for believing the mirror

i have tried so desperately

to not reflect in.

A BEDTIME STORY

There were three shovels in the bed. One shovel was made of glass and adorned by roses growing on a vine, the way roses don't. One shovel threw up thirty times. The other shovel said, "Don't laugh at me when I'm mad at you." This is how we started to make the garden. The onions, if punctured, would prove to be erupting with ants. The strawberries bled blue blood on planets that weren't ours, but here they did nothing extraordinary, except grow and die quietly. We don't ask for much from plants, really, just to grow and die when and where we say so. The arugula whispered constitutions for the country of the lonesome, and the Fourth of July got us all so excited that the forest set itself on fire. That's where the shovels come in, again. Weaving through sonic waves to the rescue, raining down from helicopters with red crosses, plunging into graves for the forest which was something much worse than dead; a changed state. You, but not you, but all that I have of you, placed the planks in a fine rectangle that wasn't a square (although a square is a rectangle) and filled it with bones that weren't sand (although sand is bones) and we ate the corpse baby tomatoes with teeth of knives and most importantly hands of shovels and we went to bed, though a bed is not a grave (although a grave is a bed).

A Salad

I cordially invite you, Melody Ruediger, to a fruit party.
Curl up in a melon wedge,
honey dew, bring a book.
Don't worry about being sticky, honey, do
you want to hold the melon baller?
Divots for your elbows and hips and wine glass.
Those grapes who didn't come together are peeling their skins
to touch eyeballs in the upstairs bedroom,
purple layers of rice paper braiding towards the door.
The bad seeds are on the porch doing blow and talking about their mothers,
they were all too pitted to stay in.
Watermelon's in the kitchen full of holes but still standing, you know how it is.
Two years ago lemon met lime and now they're both crying.
It could be the sour sting in their eyes,
could be because
they are exactly where they are supposed to be.
Give lime some salt and tequila and she'll sing you the blues the pinks AND the reds.
Apples, those pink ladies in the living room, dancing on a floor of banana peels,
trying to smash squelch and orgy into apple sauce.
The music sounds like sunlight on peach shoulders
but grapefruit keeps trying to play "Morning in the Kitchen"
(because she knows ALL the words).
Consumption and transformation of the orange—   sorrow.
Mourning in the kitchen. Orange bled red through rows of rind teeth.
By sunrise, a front yard of smoothie and dust,
a blender, cigarette butts, a spoon by the door—

and a bowl of piano keys in the living room.

STILL & ALL

"Still"
adjective, still·er, still·est.
   "remaining in place or at rest; motionless;   stationary"[1]

Give us your prayers, and we will deliver them.
Give us your prayers, and we will take them to God
by satellite, to the origin point of the big bang,
the last known location of God.

When electromagnetism was detected by multiple receivers across Earth's surface,
it was discovered that the blast which occurred 14 billion years ago is still occurring,
the primordial cosmic background, the radiation of
a Beginning,
not ours,
alone,
but ours,
in one way,
or another.

still (n.2)
circa 1200, "a calm," from **still** (adj.). Sense of "quietness, the silent part"
is from c. 1600 (*in still of the night*).[2]

Give us your prayers, and we will tell you that
God is a suicide bomber, exploding himself to give birth to the Universe.
God's sacrifice is still permeating through our bones,
God is still throwing the stars further and further from
themselves, the celestial sky is receding, our children's children's children's
children *(infinitum)* will look up at a swallowed black heaven,
the stars only myths of stories of entities.
What statue could we erect to immortalize the star?
Could these punctures in the dark sheet of the Universe be forgotten for good ?
When will a new Beginning become us?
Nothing can Be, forever. In the same way, it is.

---

[1] Still. (n.d.). Retrieved from https://www.dictionary.com/browse/still
[2] Still (adj.). (n.d.). Retrieved from https://www.etymonline.com/word/still

quietness, the silent part.
I wouldn't die for the stars.
But I would live for them.

"Gravity" is the warping of space.
The Universe is bending, breaking, becoming,
and gravity would be God, if prayers could sink.

Give me your prayers, and I will promise you
gravity, which interacts not just on mass,
but on energy.   Do you wish to be pulled close
                                        to the people you love, forever?

Examples of "still life"
The third painting was a still life of four oranges and a pear, with a brown coffee pot.
                                        from Cambridge English Corpus[3]

Give me your prayers, and I will promise
a silent reception. Sound is the vibration of air, but in space,
there's no air for sound to travel *through*.
In space, no one can hear you scream.
But a whisper of belief, of hope,
the Universe might bend her ears
to listen.

still
adjective
\ 'stil \
Definition of *still*
1   a   :"not effervescent"
      b   : "uttering no sound"[4]

'Effervescence' is when gas escapes water. Nothing escapes stillness.

The speed of light is 670,000,000 miles per hour.
Time stops, at the speed of light.

---

[3] STILL LIFE | definition in the Cambridge English Dictionary. (n.d.). Retrieved from
https://dictionary.cambridge.org/us/dictionary/english/still-life
[4] Still. (n.d.). Retrieved from https://www.merriam-webster.com/dictionary/still

Approaching the speed of light, time is experienced as slower
and slower.

Both body mass and metabolic rate determine how different animals perceive
time. The smaller the body, the faster the system, the slower and more
intricately time exists for these organisms. The hummingbird's heart beats
1,260 times a minute.

Time is perceived at its finest resolution by the quickening of the heart.

This makes sense, given the first time I realized I was *in* love

I was within love, the world spun slower, wind rested, our youth so prolonged.
I was looking at you, under the blankets we had dragged to the roof above my
mom's garage, I was looking at you sleeping, breathing small sounds, and
when your eyes slipped open, your lips parted, and you reached for me,
I thought *"Oh, I am in love."*
It was twilight, then, always, when your presence in my thoughts
prompted my heart to run towards the speed of light.
Being in love propels the body into the mind of a hummingbird,
where the world has more time to unfold.

still
Idioms
    still and all, nonetheless; even with everything considered:[5]

Thus, I write in defense of "still," a concept that has been mauled by the
understanding of absolute perpetual motion of all matter and energy in the
Universe. Some have concluded that "Still" does not exist, because "Still" is
relative to the degree at which we perceive it, the rate of time at which the World
occurs. A mountain is "still" in relation to the clouds, if seen from a distance, and
only for a short time, a human time, of maybe some hours. But the mountain
is stretching, sinking, building and crumbling, "still" exists, but "still" doesn't
mean 'lack of movement," it means a *temporal perception of relativity.*

---

[5] Still. (n.d.). Retrieved from https://www.dictionary.com/browse/still

Nonetheless, even with everything considered, the world was still when I was in love. It hurt, it dizzied, the speeding up and crumbling of all the needed "truths" that made our love last. Until it didn't. Now, poetry is the only thing that can open the portal into my past stillnessess.

Again, you are the boy living in the attic, and I am sixteen, sitting on my kitchen floor, waiting for you to slow the clocks.

:still
adverb
2   *archaic*

a : ALWAYS, CONTINUALLY[6]

Give us your prayers, and we will promise the
eternal youth of light beams, if we could move at the speed of light,
time would never stop, the truest "still"
is only reached at an impossible velocity.
As prayers approach the speed of light,
their mass becoming infinite, heavier and heavier
until the sky drops them like bombs.

still
intransitive verb
1

b : "to put an end to"[7]

A star is exploding exactly one million light years from your cheek.
For a moment, everything is stilled
by this dying light kissing your face.
It is unclear how I know the star is exploding
right now, but sometimes you have a feeling a death is occuring
in front of you, you feel the goodbye before it is uttered,
you grieve before the casket
drops.
I will see the star for years after you're gone, from whatever is going to kill you,
like lung cancer or an overdose or your father.

---

[6] Still. (n.d.). Retrieved from https://www.merriam-webster.com/dictionary/still

[7] Still. (n.d.). Retrieved from https://www.merriam-webster.com/dictionary/still

But for now I am
still
even though everyone and everything is dying or going to die, I am
still
[stil]
(synonyms for *still*)

halcyon, serene, hushed[8]

I am still
in defense of   still

[8] "still" Thesaurus.com! (n.d.). Retrieved from https://thesaurus.com/browse/still

A POWERLESS GOD

Jesus died for the sins of humanity   nails through palm   wooden spine
     the terror of the carpenter's fate-   to *become* the furniture   he had once mastered.
       Jesus couldn't have known the gravity of

the sins   to come.

another Summer of charred hills   blood crusted skies   tree bones protrude
              mid July   blistered river skin
'the beginning' is only visible in hindsight   we're much too far to turn away
       yet heads swivel toward memories of   Simple
       we look back,   our loved ones calcified into pillars of salt
our own bodies   waterless crystallizations   sand and gasoline statuettes
     we look backward   forward   and straight up and we see   *red.*

       barefoot marching and bloody balls of feet   shake the windows
   of our house   curtains drawn   the victims of the drought   flood the streets
protestors of the apocalypse   demanding the heads of dead men   someone must
       body the blame
for this Earth death   but we look backward   forward   and straight up and we see
     it is *us*   whose hands   are wet with   red
   but we too, come out   with parchment paper tongues   and bleached eyes
       walking proudly on our knees   demanding water from God.

in our final masterpiece   humans found a way to conquer the sky
   to burn the clouds   to press oil from our corpses   so the hearse may feed
so the hearse may carry   burnt boiled or buried, we become the ash
          we had once mastered.

   the hands of the healer   grow punctures in centers of palms
   no trees   to build a cross   no martyr to save us   from
   the Final Page   of People   of Power   of Pillaging   of Pride   of Praying
          Praying needs

          Fear.

   we turn the page   to find our role   in the End of things

". . . the last thing to go —

crucified — Hope."

God is always configured as   the power   to do   what you can't.
why ask God   when you're not even sure   your voice   makes noise   why speak
for no purpose   but to hear yourself
say what you fear:

SAY WHAT YOU FEAR

say what
or who
you are powerless   to.

SPEAK

I heard you late last night.
Maybe they were walking in unison, the people you keep
in your head, straining floorboards with heels and toes.
I heard 100 footsteps belonging to 1 or 2 or 6 people
I heard one of them tell you that you are a bad daughter
and I heard two of them agree.
Over the sound of the song I am sick of
nauseously on repeat,
I hear your knives preparing the dinner your mother taught you
hear your knives rusting in the sink
hear your knives ripping porcelain
hear your knives butchering meat
hear your knives finding their way
into your veins
hear pills clambering to escape from their cages
hear the creaking of your jaw as I pry open your mouth with two chop-
sticks
hear my voice invading the tranquility of your evaporation
Hear my voice! Hear it!
I hear my voice and you do not
I hear my voice and I am alone
I heard you last night
talking in your sleep
about how you know he doesn't Love you
doesn't Need you.
I heard you say he doesn't really need you.
I hear my voice—

        "but I need you"

    I hear my voice

    but you do not

    I didn't hear the bathtub running, was too busy taping "I love you"s
to all the mirrors didn't hear the rope knotting, was too busy drowning your
sharp objects in velvet didn't hear you slipping through my fingers, too busy
trying to build your world more solid.

I hear you try to kill my best friend and
I hear you both say
in unison

     "Wait
          we didn't mean it"

but this time
it was, I was,
too late.
I don't hear you
I don't hear anything

because it is late,

and
it
is
too   late .

How-To

Bury me in a bed of bleached processed sugar
        and fill my mouth with pink salt (himalayan pink salt).
When I'm pretending to love you,
        I'm soaking my feet in red wine and painting my eyes interested.

Call me when you get home safe and call me when
        you don't.
Quiet feet and a paranoid brain
        I am untouchable,
painfully so.

It's hard to throw away the Armor
        but I'm still a soldier when I am naked,
I'm just less of a good one.
        How do these shirts fit over the fingers growing from my ribs,
how do you hold my hand when I weigh less than air?

Here is the part where everyone is the hero
        and the dragon wasn't who you thought she was
(red footprints up and down the walls).
        The wine poisoned my nails and they look so beautiful but please
whisper they can't know that in sickness they are lovely

                                        just lovely
                            just

I want to forget my body or unfold into yours
        but my hands leave Play-Doh smudges down your chest
 Before Me, you were the cleanest thing I'd ever seen
        the unread-newspaper walls of your lungs
void of smeared or loving ink.

There's no angel or idol or statue unblemished
by the hands or the teeth or the sun.
        We lasted a grape's life, from birth to rot in months,
just say we had a year,

say we had one good year.

Lucy said the doormat uses the user
     and that it's complicated
but I do not think it is complicated
     and that maybe she just wishes it was.

People who win the lottery commit suicide at an alarming rate:
     getting all that you've asked for
and finding yourself still alone,
     in the house you used to share.

The apple's armor, the teeth laced with skin, when I'm pretending to love you,
     I am the doormat, using my user, making Us complicated.
The dragon the princess and the hero:
     all one name under my tongue.

PEACH JAM

I don't know if we came here for something
why we became so animal.
shoulder blades pressed into the floor of the riverbank
palms empty, staring down humidity,
perspiring gold,
the potential for renewal buzzing across our skin- why?
the sky is empty, except for us.
tired pearls of sweat stretch their limbs across my upper lip
my body slides off herself,
melts into cobblestone cracks,
slinks between two or four legs. desire
has little to do with reality,
desire is only what has not yet
occurred.
I can taste the Want
it drags one finger down my neck over my ribs past my hips
Peach Jam all
over the front page,
I forgive you for being so sweet and
blurring my words
and for still Taking me when I'm
slurring my words—
I only wanted to be able to love you in a different language
to be able to sit at your parents' dinner party and say
"queiro tenerte.
Encuéntrame
en tu cuarto de niño."
your family will laugh nervously with incomprehension.
I'll tell you what to do
with a tone that sounds like "come help me find my wallet"
and their ears will be unable to digest the proof of our quiet desire.

IRON

My daughters and I will weep on the First Day of our cycle,
we mourn the tides of bloody shrapnel pulled out of us
by the moon. It's not just blood; it is the acidic scarlet skin,
the ripped crimson curtains, the drapery of budding rot.
On the First Day, we weep
because our uncles can't touch us anymore
because now, they want to
because now, driving by the cows in the field makes our tits sore,
and the absence of children will mean the presence of blood,
clotted scrambles of acidic innards, the detritus of potential life.
As the uterine wine paints pure cotton canvas,
our fingers fumble at the locks of chastity belts,
hoping to hide the embarrassing evidence of fertility.
Blood-stained sheets cry the crime of murdered childhood.
In a time without Modern medicine, our skirts smiled
at the possible birth of a rape kit,
the honest truth of the flesh,
the organism-receipt of inception, a shitting, babbling I-told-you-so,
             to prove all the semen.
                          A baby born to a virgin?
                          Then it must have been God in the hands of her pants.
Immaculate deception.
Some miracles are just lies,
but red,
red doesn't lie.
    The panties passively await the ejaculation of biological destiny,
relief comes, but fear...   the red begs the question...
             will you   ever   produce
                          anything   but this iron wreckage?
A canvas vomited upon by the unconscious second-hand,
    Purpose   inscribed in rust,
the hour glass emptying...
the condemnation reads:
                          And this month,
                          for your crimes,
                      of having bared no fruit,
                      Today you bleed, Bitch.

SWEET

Raspberry scone laying across my tongue
I think about how she must taste
like fruit sugar wrapped in swollen dough.
I think about his tongue sliding between folds of pink pastry
I think about the day-olds
remembered in plastic memory. No one can be preserved.
I heard he made her cum with his mouth
and quietly remembered how I never even let him
kiss me in front of our friends.
Here, I scarf their trail of breadcrumbs
that leads towards their honeymoon cabin in the woods
where he wolfs, waits,
for a girl in red.
A girl, like a young girl, one that is honored to be asked to enter
a Story about Caution.
I devoured the bread that reminded me of her.
Anything that looked Innocent is, at my age, buried deep inside my bowels
But she will hunger soon
and he will move to fresher bread
full price, no discount.
Maybe then,
I will share a coffee with her, a cigarette,
some food no one had to die to make.
We will wonder if this is Victory:
to become the pages
left out of his book.

PINOCCHIO

I walked into the doctor's office
my knees knocking and shadows blinding my eyes.
The white coat sat me down, asked if I was an only child,
asked if I was excitable, asked if I was dumb.
The white coat diagnosed me with floating triangles.

She prescribed me drywall, icicles, and an umbrella.
She prescribed me rage
and a pot to boil in.

A mobile of daggers orbited me a halo.
I tried painting the triangles, to make them look like less of a disease,
a bashful monarch butterfly. I tied pigeons to my Pinocchio limbs,
a swarm to mask my hovering shame,
my posture now elongated by strings tied to pigeons in flight.
The triangles sound like a silverware drawer
when they collide with the wings.
A walking chandelier of sharp and soft
clattering down the sidewalk, birds crying and shitting uncontrollably
a mobile of growths, cysts, spreading...
The mold of the world held by strings.

The pigeons are nocturnal, roosting on the windowsill while I sleep.
The triangles move like blades.
The triangles don't sleep.

Though a monarch may only speak its poison through orange,
I realized those who tasted me would still sense the silent sickness.
The triangles move through wings like water.
Waiting at the bus stop,
I saw one of the pigeons had been pierced through the heart
by the 30-degree angle of an isosceles.
I dragged her dead weight for three blocks
before realizing her heart had stopped.
The string between us wouldn't cut from my shoulder,
so she tattered behind me like wedding bells
until the concrete shredded her Free.

forgive me
I never meant for my pain to suffocate such beautiful things
but there is only so much space
in the
                    air

STICKING HEADS IN THE SAND

A hurricane and a flood head for the west coast.

How was your summer? How was your trip?
Did you fall in love?
Did you swim a lot?
Did you make new friends?
Did you keep writing?
What was the highlight? What was your rapist's name?
        You don't remember? You can't say it?
Was it rape-rape? Are you pressing charges?
Do you still like to fuck? Did you go on any hikes?
    Did you keep writing? Did you work a lot?
swapping trauma like pokemon cards
summer loves and sexual assaults
adventures and attacks
from heads pushed into sand   to bruises discovered in the morning, but no memory
            no memory
of being in a fist   fight
So what happened?
How was your summer?
Did you wear sunscreen? Did you keep writing?
Did you go to the pool? Is he a serial or solo-incident kinda guy?
Did the police believe you? Did the doctors?
Did anyone?
Laying on our stomachs at a sleepover with wet nails we talk about
screaming and silence.
Just Girl Talk, you know.
Girl Talk.
It used to be wishing they'd notice us, now we plan where to hide.
Pillow fights in our underwear, training to fend off unwanted advances
so that next time, we'll be better prepared.
Next time.
A little file in a big folder in a big cabinet in a big room next to a thousand
other girls who "just should have stayed home that night"
intoxicated / bite-mark-bruise / hair ripped up
    torn leggings / underwear inside out . . . .
the puzzle pieces fit together but

it takes
    a little
        force
Girl
    Talk
Tell
   me

the story and Tell me until you can say it without crying the judge won't
be able to understand you they won't understand you they won't hear you
no one can fucking hear you speak the fuck up walk faster fight tougher
draw blood glare cold become hard don't break don't break don't
break IF
there was ever a time to be strong, it is now.
This is Gossip this is Girl
Talk please just Tell Me WHERE
did you GET
those panties? The ones in the evidence bag? Is pink your favorite color?
Did your mom cry when you told her? How hard?
Are your eyes glued open
or stapled shut
were you too drunk to fuck
were you too weak to fight
did your freckles darken?
Did you keep writing?
How was your summer?

      I stopped.

    A hurricane misses, but the flood comes anyway.

PART THREE

ENTOMOPHOBIA

What in your life are you most afraid of?
When the Assassin bug feeds on termites,
she will paste the corpses of the termites to her back.
The termites will rush to rescue their dying family,
and the Assassin will skewer them too.
The World punishes Love this way.
I could imagine killing you
and the thought excites me.
I would centrifuge your corpus
while your organs beat each other to a pulp
in a tornado of collisions.
I could imagine killing you,
and the thought helps me sleep at night.
I would hold you down,
I would make you say her name.
I would make you dig her up,
I would kiss her to your back.
I would drag you to the gorge,
I would bury you soundless
at the site of her reckoning,
your last breaths mocked by the heat,
your forgotten life camouflaged by her decomposition,
I want you
      powerless.
I am the assassin now, hating you
in your locked cage, jail bird,
does the weight of every woman you've slaughtered break your wings?
In victory, you are alone again, see?
The song on repeat, from the bird's beak, until he dies, is
"I hurt her to get to you" I hurt her to get to you I hurt her to get to you
I hurt her to get to you I hurt her to get to you I hurt her
to get
you
these words bloodied my hands,
you flightless bird, barking from the grave, bedroom, and penitentiary;

I heard your song until the coal mine
dissolved us,
toxins in the air,
ghost-leeches sucking scratches from walls.
Were you not born of woman?
Not born a wingless nymph?
Can a beetle kill a bird?
The birds and the bees, beetles, this was how
they said it would be, to be with another, the Assassin bug
uses a toxin to tranquilize their prey, paralyzed alive,
they suck the prey's liquified organs through straw mouths.
The prey's heart still beats while his insides begin to melt,
a handless captain aboard his own shipwreck,
watching the scene from below the ocean floor.
The bug's stomach gorges, filling herself with the other,
Take everything, Take what you will not be
given Take what you are owed
you owe me
a life.
I remember the toxins before they became mine,
the tranquilizer sedative acid bile rip bleeding vomit bite I can imagine killing you,
and the thought brings me *relief.*
Relief, of finally loosening the choke-hold you roped round my brain,
your rigamortis fingers I could crack off one by one.
  I would bury them each separately, so your hands could never find themselves,
so they could never hold her down again

   I would shred your eyes, too, unwind their tape recorder memories
and find the moment you became a bird of prey
      find the moment that made all this pain possible
   I would kill myself if I ever saw you in my reflection.

Your limbs decompose and I sow them back together, one by one,
  trying to keep your corpse human-enough to stay in the story,
    but entropy saves you again
      you mother fucking *infection*

I would whirlpool your innards to find you hollow and sucked of lifeblood,
                    your flesh frame collapses,   sack of you,   jigsaw,
            your jaw loosens,   teeth unhinge from around my wrists
        I reverse peel your tattered sheath to my back and
I will never be finished bearing your corpse,
                    it will always have been me.
                        The fish hook tugging between
                        our stories and our wounds
                        is renamed an
                        Intimacy, for the sake of   Closeness.

The adolescent Assassin bug molts four times,
shedding decayed skins of a lesser predator,
until she has died enough times to kill.
"What in your life are you most afraid of?"
and I realize, I am afraid, of myself, I am afraid
of what I am capable of, I am afraid
that I could kill a man,
and I am afraid
that I would like it.

A LITTLE DEATH

It was too heavy a little death
wedged pebbles braided into ribs.
I would never say you broke me,
but it goes without saying that I became broken,
grew into less pieces.

Here, in the little death, Mother and sister of the pride lick my wounds,
paws circle round my discarded heap, letting her pass over in peace.
My pride, pooling at my feet, the pride that needed to thaw
in order to penetrate numb:
what has been kept frozen that weighs us into matter,
condemning women to physical existence by Aristotle's decree.

I boiled the rats you promised me were crazy,
even my dreams have become domesticated.
In submission I lose my fingernails and my skin turns to rubber.

Straddling the hours you took from me,
a totem lay comatose atop your heart-broken.
I slit the mold of a woman
into bleeding plastic, first practicing on myself.

All that I needed to bury you
was *in* me,
I had it all along.

Killing you was always going to mean dying a little.

So my hands grew to shovels
and I stood with my mother beside my bed, your grave
(my mother, proud of how cruel she had built me).

We cursed what shiver was left
of the corpse I had made of you.

MARY

My picky thorn, toddler Queen
ruling this canyon of teeth,
extinct wood of mouth.

Hills wearing overgrowth of blue ferns
bleeding saltwater into cracked palms, waiting.

Your subjects awake to you overbite-screaming,
but you walk on your toes
edging the cliff of this canyon,
trying to catch your echo.
Nothing as naive as   *"Come back,"*
so the toddler Queen tantrums the sunrise back down.

These women know that Protection
is a Sanctuary of locked doors.
Sleep-walking the valley, asking for more from this Life,
these women are all those parts of you
that you couldn't save.

Your Queendom the grandest canyon,
I know you had a reason for all this mud,
once.
but you can't hide the Saved forever.
The wheezing current nudges paper prayers
messages unbottled
the tremor hands scratch into canvas
"Save us from this Blessing."
Years down the river, litter-cries wash ashore,
love letters about hating their God,
save us from heaven,
*"Let me be damned if by my own thumbs,
as long as they're mine."*

They are ungrateful in your world–
you feed them anyway.

This village of cavities and girls made of bread,
crosses penciling into retinas and the undersides of bellies.
Who would protect them, or you, if they escaped your heavy wings?
Is there a place in your pock-marked country for the threading of childhood,
a supremacy of yarn?

These women here, dolls of mud and straw,
guarded by scarecrows stuffed with bird bones.
There is the Crying you must pretend not to hear, there are
the footsteps along the walls that circle back over themselves.
There are your good intentions weeping *"How'd it get this bad?"*
        Only dust answers.

Your queens chamber built of watercolor words,
feeding a muddy river for your disciples
to drink with their hands.
They smell your perfume of honeybee wings and rose thorns
as they kneel to imbibe water
that is only Holy
because it is born from   above.

MY DEAD HUSBAND

I spilled red wine on the shoulders of my favorite book
Fitting, really
loving him to shreds, carrying around the diary of a dead man
across Europe.
I think carrying around the book of a dead person
is one of the nicest things you can do.
A pocket mouse squeaking its visions of other worlds,
animals are not allowed on the train
you only payed for one adult, ma'am.
I silence him into my bag, muffled prophecies whispering into
my lipsticks, pens, and loose change.
"Just one ticket, please."
I'm laughing tears into your paper neck because we fooled them, didn't we, B?
They think I'm alone, don't you?
The mouse teeth fall as we walk down the train corridors,
the ticking is an hourglass pulling sand from your arm like dead skin.
Carrying around the book of a dead person is one of the nicest things.
They may have died 100 years ago
but you can still lay next to them on the beach
and hear their thoughts
on Wine and Milk and Jealousy.
The death of an author creates an infinite one-way conversation.
Barthes, I know what you think about love, how it splits your brainstem
          into lover, son, brother,
god.
No one had told me about the bitterness of Love's necessity...
with you, my love, I am never less alone with someone.
Speak unto, into, the wordless blunder that fear does become.

We Have Forever

You look at your mom–
you haven't seen her in months,
for some reason (you know 'how' this happened, but the 'why' is harder)–
you look at her, sitting in the green chair,
and she's so...
old?
of course,
as you grow up,
your mother grows old.
but you look at her,
and all of the sudden,
she is the old lady you watched struggle
across the street this morning.
10
flashing red hand
   9
she's doing her best, moving as fast
as she can she's walking across the street,
doing her best
somebody should help
her flashing   red
       8
she's the woman with grey roots and red
hair, arthritis tape wrapped around her wrists,
bagging your fucking groceries at the supermarket.
she lifts jars with her mummy paws,
an imperceptible wince behind her eyes,
why couldn't you have bought less things, lighter things,
a gentle gesture would be to help her, no, it'd be much gentler
to read her name off her name-tag, to say it with care, why
these flashing, red, hands,
hurry,
        7
she's the woman looking at the newspaper with a fucking
microscope, her hands are shaking the paper
so bad, it wouldn't matter if the words were exit-sign leg legible, she's
earthquaking the words from ever reaching her retinas

she can't I could
help her
hands

6

flashing

your mother is sitting in that damn green chair,
flipping through channels on her dresser,
she's mouthing the words to her shows, the family in the frames
are silent, she says the remote is broken, it can't go off

    mute

the cat on her lap died three days ago, she hasn't moved,
the left paw is falling off whirring TV faces upside-down,
eyes
somebody!

       red hands

flashing across the walls I don't speak to her
I *recite.*

      she can't remember so much
these days

5

she's the limping dog you saw at the edge of the field, left hind leg
bleeding, grey whiskers she's so thin, so thin, rice paper skin, and you say

      "don't you belong to someone?"

and you know she can't hear you

4

her father couldn't remember
so much

      (red)

he looks at you, you are 10 years-old, he says "Christine, I love you"
you say "my name is Gwen"
he says "I know my own daughter's name"

3

you help her into bed she does not look into your eyes
you put a pillow between her legs, she is grateful, and this
kills

you

she

says "I am so tired of fighting"
        and you,
        you say nothing.

        and then,

        you leave.

                                        2

she is sitting in the green chair

and you haven't seen her in months,
                                flashing in and out,
                and you look at her,

                                                1

    and you know, outside on the street, the red hand is flashing, but
Time shows you both mercy, for once.

    She is asleep with the light still on, book in hand, you are crawling
into bed beside her, she is asking if you had a bad dream
and "I miss you" wouldn't cut it, but you let yourself say it anyway,
and you are nine years old
again,

and she lets you belong to someone

and you look at her
                and she is the woman anchoring your orbit in a world off-kilter,
    softly snoring with moonlight pooling through orange curtains,
her warm, steadied hands, freckled velvet skin.
                And you know,
you both know, that one of you will die first, one of you will die alone,
and both of you will die many times over.

If no amount of time could profess a gratitude of such depth,
 then this endless distance,
  never quite eclipsed
 to be as close as when I lived within your every step,
our flashing eternity and escaping bliss,
 it is enough.

A Room with No Exits

I.
It is made by measurements of air, word boxes you can crawl into,
one for crying, one for talking through your fingers,
one for insomnia.
With orbits unhinged, what connects the hair to the skin?
Your exit signs misplaced onto footprints,
exit signs of when and where and how you left,
I track these losses in search
of a less offensive fuel than crude oil,
but the dirt tastes the same when it crawls back out.
A room with no exits, like the grave digger
consumed by her own labor, 10 feet under
held by walls of a final resting place, walls
mourning the eviction of tenant soil,
now a box to be filled by rain, remains.
Somewhere in the landfill of last night
I found you buried alive
a flower in one fist
and something that won't decompose
in the other.

II.
There won't ever be a name for you.
I believe the words weightless enough to stick to you
evaporated like sighs of water
toward crow wings.
If everything left a trail
we could land all the planes and tell everybody to go home,
go home, whatever you're looking for, I promise, it's between two things,
not somewhere you could land a plane,
not something you could capture or sustain.
Go home, search instead for the ripples
of where stone punctured surface,
the body of water bears no exit wound,
where does the body end?
The migrations of lovers and seasons
rely on trails, on the opacity and
brainlessness of wind.
You were always too anxious to be good
at swing dancing, too preoccupied wondering
if you'd done the last step wrong to focus
on getting this

                one

              right.
You were so hesitant of life.
Your exits come to me in a memory:
our kitchen floor covered in two inches of water,
my lighthouse, the jar of honey
by the window,
the salt and sugar altar of unrequited remembrance.
"regardless," "without regard," or "despite something,"

      Love doesn't have to feel like this.

I can't remember what your face looks like
and I will continue to say that
until it is true.

III.

When the crows come to eat my eyes out
I want you to know that I probably fell asleep
with the window open.
My prize was lying comatose with palms facing clouds,
exhaling the unspeakable knots from my throat.
What I would give to be pinned to the ceiling,
to shut my window eyes,
to let my lungs savor air and free my joints from their puzzles.
What I would give to pass through something with no exits,
to pass through a body like a disease,
         or Spring.
Sitting with wrists of paper, white paint flaking off rot teeth,
I find the words
    somewhere between the stem and the fruit,
where all perfect things live.
Tomorrow I am without tongue, yesterday without mind, yet
here is this *somewhere*
of perfect, staggering clarity–
Something I can surround with words like shadow to color.
The painter says, "You need shadow for depth."
An adumbration like the penumbra–
Penumbra, of the Latin word *paene*, meaning "almost, nearly."
The region between shadow and not, partial eclipse,
for a moment, neither, where the indescribable occurs.
The region shadowed into existence, touching two places at once, existing in neither.
The heart of the poem is the echo
bouncing off and in between the crude lines of language.
The best part of the poem, the best part of our story, is
the words left out.

I MISSED CHURCH THIS SUNDAY

Jesus, how do I   stop?
I don't want to be on God's mailing list anymore,
prayer magnets pulling my knees to the ground
when I can barely stand.
I can barely stand. So I missed church, forgot to be saved,
                  I miss being saved.

              But I don't want to be held in all-forgiving arms
              today.
Don't bless my sins, Don't color this violence
anything but senseless, Don't give this wound
a rhyme / a reason / a righteous justification god
damn Jesus
        it's not all forgivable,
                    it's not.
        Someone needs to tell you that you can't save everyone,
                      you can't.

Forgive *yourself*, Father
for knowing who you can't save.
Let us identify ourselves to you,
let me unroot my hell and fall to my knees on my   own.

I appreciate getting mail, I do.
But some troubles don't float away on faith—
it takes something like a *current*,
and I've tried, but these
faults and holy water pass through my fingers:
I can't hold humanity this tight
without strangling.

I miss being saved, being forgiven,
but it has to be possible to let go
of what is already gone.

FOR ANNA

I will be brave like
this furry critter Olympus padding my collarbone with mitten paws
curling her tail around my elbow
meandering to our sunroom to stare at our neighbor opening his trunk
to retrieve an empty stroller, brave like
forgetting, for a single moment,
that there is somewhere and someone you are supposed to be.
But if living so happily was not brave enough
we also fed ourselves, forgave our parents, freckled our cheekbones and palms,
stopped giving bruises on our shins stories, stopped remembering
the words we could not forgive, we stopped and can I tell you it felt so good
    to let go?
Can I tell you about all the goodness?
the smoked salmon with capers on crackers,
the "$15 and under" wine rack at Mr. Lee's corner store,
the lazy orange coating the kitchen of my childhood home,
the riverbed that becomes a whirlwind of golden plankton when she is touched,
the darkest parts of a mother's heart,
what is left in one's hair once the creek's veins have evaporated.
For the Things That Want to Happen
when no more words can be said,
no more lines can be drawn,
the circle running over itself, just remember:
'quiet' is not silenced, 'fragile' is beyond breakable,
    it is brave.
It is okay that you are tired.
Just because you can't describe it
doesn't mean it's not happening *I know*
it takes so much bravery to lose—
he perdido, he estado perdiendo, the loss remains
in the imperfect, too, because
'loss' is an Always Occurrence, 'loss' is
what never got to happen,
and despite all of it
we are still living in the moments that Did.

that Are.
Bravery is "Being, despite it all"
even if all you're doing
is looking out your sunroom window, or
staying in this moment
just a little bit
longer.

HEREDITARY

I wanted to make something that couldn't touch the ground.
Instead of acknowledging that there is a lineage of pain
in how we are made, I ask where I wouldn't be
if I hadn't spent all those years
trying to make myself worthy of Love.

I wanted to make something that couldn't touch the ground.

I quieted the wasps from drinking my shadow, but I didn't take lessons from their
still wings.
I didn't ask why they had come for me,
why now.
Why come, when I hadn't sent for them?
They told me stories about the world that hurt my ears, they told me about
my family, my grandmother split in half
over a french bathtub, my grandfather levitating
above the basement carpet like a magic trick.
    Is my lineage a warning, or a threat?
I swallowed the wasps into a corked jug lined with honey, buried them alive,
and forgot the jug deep somewhere I would never allow myself
to see.

How do I build a child out of love?
With no hands, no Gods, no sense of architecture

I see myself at 35, I am, 35, and I want to be the mother
I didn't have. I manifest what I think is Creation,
imagine "New," imagining "New."
New, I'm pregnant, tickling my stomach, whispering prayers about
pink and rosemary and forgiveness, and I feel it in me.
(There is no father, of course. We both know why.)

Then there is the urgency, to let it come. I want to make something that can't
        touch the ground.
    my sweat   pushes
through   pores

28 hours of
Labor. To be obedient
to your body, your flesh frame is taking notes of what you
won't let yourself see.

My midwife kneels between my legs, saying 'it's supposed to hurt.'
My midwife, my bringer of Earth, saying to 'let it out.'
My midwife saying 'you're going to be alone in your body again'
My midwife lifts the weight from in and under me, from out of me saying
'here
it
comes!!'

no sounds

My eyes sweat, throat
trembles
mouth cracks—
she can't look away
from *what* is in her hands.

She has pulled from within me
a corked jug
bloated with wasp corpses.
She raises the offering of my sex, her forearms dipped in velvet oil.
The jug pulses behind its skin-membrane, the surface slick with
the lubricant that runs between dead and alive.
She doesn't say a thing,
just stands, eyeing me wearily.
Pity, or compassion, I can't tell.
The message in the bottle is spoken without words,
a sound so small it slips through the cracks of her teeth.
I reach my arms out to hold *It.*

I wanted to make something the ground couldn't touch.
She shakes her head,
and,
moving like last-words,
carries the bundle, my attempt at Life, to the fifth floor balcony ledge.

She looks at me once more, my body ripped apart by hereditary insects.

"You are contagious," she says.

Then steps into the sky.

THE TENDENCY OF ALL THINGS TOWARDS TOGETHERNESS

The water unmelting into something that can break
skulls, glacier unfreezing unborn. All the pages flutter
their retreat up the creek, the uncurrent, undoing themselves
back into the barren spine, nestling themselves in chronological order,
and thus,
it is written.
My nose is bleeding before you punch me,
then blood licks itself back to my brain, or absorbs
into your knuckles.

The second law of Thermodynamics is the Law of Entropy

The water unspills from my bedside table, unfloods the only photo I have
of you, and I didn't even take the picture. The room I left this morning,
tobacco whiskers, eyelid powder, petal mummies,
it undoes itself back to order, contained piles.
Your hands, shoving, instead pull me up
from the lawn, invisible strings, I unbruise, ungasp,
the back of my head unhits
the concrete.

Entropy is the arrow of time. Every simplicity is destined for chaos.

The water ungives life, unmakes the Earth
special, unfills the basins of every vein.
My grandmother's body undecomposes just in time for Mother's Day, limbs
reattached by memory of amputation, it was here,   here   and   *here*.
My trust is unbroken, ungiven, unformed.
The baby chick in my brothers hands melts back into a white/yellow dichotomy,
unhatching, eggshells click back together round the fluid fetus.

Entropy is the only fundamental rule of physics that is time-sensitive.

The water is unmaking itself, the green plate picks herself off the floor,
braiding pieces into a whole. You unsay the words
"Why can't you let anything be *simple*"

I unhear those words, I unremember them,
I undwell on how complicated I make
every story.

I unwrite this poem, and something finally happens, for good.

THERE ARE MANY WAYS TO TELL THIS STORY II

The poems are written
   before they occur to me.
      Something about a scar, something about a hymn.

Vacancy promises creation,
   for only in a vacuum
      can a Deity or Universe be born.

Poetry is a prolonged glance,
   direct eye-contact with the present.
      The poems are written before they are words.

I will write one, unshareable poem,
   and I will let it die with me, simple and
      forever, folded neatly in my throat.

Acknowledgments

"Cradle" appeared in the 54th edition of *Jeopardy Magazine*.

An early version of "How-To" appeared in the January 2017 issue of *The Oregon Voice*.

Thank you to Jane Wong for helping me shape the body of this collection, and for teaching both myself and my work infinite grace and wisdom. I truly don't know where I would be without your mentorship. Thank you for putting so much labor and attentiveness into this project.

Thank you to Larry Moore of Broadstone Books, for walking me through the publishing process over the past year and a half.

Thank you to Leah Cromett, for creating the cover art of my dreams. Five years ago we worked together on our high school's literary magazine, and I'm so grateful to be collaborating again with such a unique, brilliant artist. Your work is phenomenal.

Thank you to Anna Del Savio for the author photograph, copy editing, and endless support.

If you want to look at more of Leah's art, find her on instagram: @morcleha.

ABOUT THE AUTHOR

Gwen Frost is the author of this book, and no other books. After winning first-place in the Oregon slam-poetry competition *Verselandia* in 2015, Gwen studied poetry and political theory at Western Washington Honors College. *Somewhere between the Stem & the Fruit* is her first full-length publication. Gwen is now living in Portland, Oregon where she is working on her next book, and taking a deep breath.